To: Dr. Sohl

Charlotte Guegan

it's okay to be afraid of the dark

charlotte guegan

for myself
thank you for inspiring me
to be true to me

trigger warning:

this book
contains
troubling content
relating to:

various forms of abuse
trauma
substance abuse
sexual assault
self-harm
homophobia
racism
alcoholism
scars
mental illness
fire
death

remember your
limits while
reading this book

contents

spoiler I:
the lesson is only a girl
learning to accept herself
as she is

spoiler II:
there is a ~~happy ending~~ new beginning
ahead

vulnerability
has been
the most difficult challenge
of my being

these pages contain
my fears
my feelings
my passions
and my epiphanies

i am laying before you
emotionally
undressed

this is my soul
on paper

I.   passion

pas·sion

/ˈpaSHən/

noun

strong and barely controllable emotion.

the seat beside me at my table is prepared. fork and knife. shiny plate. bright table cloth. it has no name card and no reservation. but it is prepared for you. you're sitting at a different table now, so people filter through this seat, it welcomes them but isnt meant for them. i am in no rush for you to sit in this seat, because i know, and you know, that this will forever be your seat beside me.

i look at your flaws
and in its place
all is see is beauty

which of us will be the sun
and which will be the moon?

there are countless meataphors that the greatest writers have
formulated to express their love
but none of them begin to capture the feelings i feel for you

you touched me before you even lifted your hands

i would rather do nothing with you
than everything with anybody else

i learned to love your words
before i learned to love the body that spoke them

hold me so close that i'm not sure where i end and you begin
hold me so close that we stop looking for ends and beginnings and
decide
just to be

i admire the way your eyes tell the stories
that your heart has kept under lock and key

and then we fell into a pool of intimacy
from which we never resurfaced
and that is okay
because you are the only air i need

you know my heart
what makes it speed up
what makes it sink
you know what upsets me
what excites me
you know whats wrong before i open mouth
you know me
and i know you

we are not two halves that make a whole
we are two wholes that only lift each other higher

we are tall on our own
but we are taller together

if this feeling i have for you is the one they call insanity
i hope to never be sane again

there is no definition of woman
other than to identify as one
a man is in no position to tell me how to act, or how to dress
just as a bird is in no position to tell a fish how to swim
your stereotypical, average standard for what a woman should look
like
is not the cast that i have to mold myself to fit into
it is time that you learn
that nobody has been put on this world
with the only objective to be your entertainment
spend your youthful years being sexualized by the education
system for having your shoulders out
spend your youthful years being a survivor of sexual assualt, only
to be told that you were asking for it, because you were wearing a
skirt
experience inequity only because you have a larger chest and
different organs
and i will listen to your ignorant standards of who a woman should
be

i know how you're feeling before a sound rolls off your lips
i know what you're going to say, with only a moment of our eyes
meeting

-   *the best conversations are the ones with no words*

just because i cannot call you mine
does not mean you cannot call me yours

-     i will always be *for* you

i dont want a love to save me from my demons
i want a love that plants seeds of security
and sticks around to watch them bloom

i've told you i love you
without using those words
in more ways than i've ever been able to tell anybody else

they pierced the holes in my wings
to ensure i could never fly anywhere ever again
so she crafted me new wings from her sweat and blood
and i stole every stare as i soared above the crowd of people who
said i couldn't

- *thank you*

i want to teach a healing woman how to save herself from her
demons
the way that you taught me to save me from mine

i will not try to save you
instead, i will teach you how to build stepping stones
from the rocks they threw at you
i will teach you how to build a pathway of love
from the remnants of a shattered reflection
that told you
you weren't enough

when the rains of my burdens
begin to blend in with my tears
you are the umbrella that keeps me dry

how can i be this attracted to somebodys soul
and not want to hold them in a romantic way?

- *platonic soulmates*

you are held down by the weight of your past
you carry it with you in a large black suitcase
everywhere you go
because you are afraid to let go
you are afraid to release this suitcase
that you continue to let define you
because you are so terrified of the unknown
terrified of having a life of freedom and bliss
not because you don't want it
but because you are so comfortable with the suit case of your past
the suitcase of who you used to be
that you dont want to know what could be
its time to drop the suitcase
cut yourself loose from the weight of the past
for you have no control over that
it is time to trade in your large black suitcase
and collect the shiny golden key to the future

a life stuff stuck on loop could never amount to a life that never
stops living

kindness is fixing another queens crown
compassion is fixing another queens crown, without letting the
world know it was crooked

the day that the sun
does not rise
will be the first day
i do not love you

- *but the sun will always rise, wont it?*

your perfume smells like home
but to the rest of the world
it smells only of vanilla

- *the smell of your sweatshirt makes my heart pound*

i am an open book
but around me there are walls built so high
even the clouds can't pass
then something about the delicate undertones
of your soft voice
turns every brick to rubble

when all the stars fall you will see

i wonder which parts of me are *mosaics* of you?

you might not have been in the sequel to the book of my love
but you were the star of every chapter you were in

the people who look at you with concern
and nod their head
and furrow their eyebrows
the people who try to understand
the people who really listen to what you're saying
the people who are there in your time of need

they are the people who i don't see anymore
and they are the people who saved me
from me

why would you be embarrassed to be vulnerable
when it is the best reflection of strength
no part of exposing yourself
should make you feel weak

and suddenly those sappy love songs
were written for me and you

they are silent to the lack of veteran recognition
until the queer community celebrates their pride
they are silent to their police appreciation
until we chant black lives matter

you allow veterans and first responders to live in the shadows
where they lay unrecognized
until a trans woman wants the same rights as a cis woman
or a black man wants the same opportunities as a white man

you do not care about veterans
you're not standing behind them to support them
you're standing behind them to shield your transphobic and rasist
ways

you only say blue lives matter in response to black lives matter
you only notice the people who fight for you
in response
because the demand for equality makes you uncomfortable

a moan is not a yes
you laugh when you are tickled
even if it hurts
and you would rather be anywhere but there
you could be screaming and crying
but you would still hear a laugh

just because she is moaning
doesnt mean she wants it

she could've invited you to her house
she could've taken her bra off
leaned in for the kiss
or unbuttoned her pants
but the moment she changes her mind
the moment she says
"stop"
"i'm uncomfortable"
is the same moment
that you should realize

your orgasm is not more important
than the level of respect she gives herself
and the level of respect she will expect from others

asking a girl why she didn't scream for help
is the same thing as telling a girl in a skirt that she was asking for it

- *silence still means no*

accepting the difficult emotions
that demand to be noticed
is the only way for their strength to lessen

the feeling of your skin against mine
establishes a peace that has been absent in me

my goal has never been to live forever
my goal has always been to create something that will live forever

i
will
never
love
another
soul
more
than
the
person
i
call
my
best
friend

there is passion in our hearts that longs to be expressed through our
tongues

the volume of your whisper
is equivalent to that of the sirens of our love

i am deaf to all but your song

i was once an unlit candle

i am now the fire you beg for
as the night grows cold
and the stars you beg for
as the sky falls dark

- *to the girl who held the match*

the world owes you every stare and every blessing she continues to
gift to you

she owes you everything and more
just for breathing this air

i spend my life trying to figure out where each peice fits
but a moment of eye contact with you
and the puzzle solves itself

you proved to me that i am not just a ball of fire
you showed me that i am a sky full of unique stars
you showed me that i am an infinity universe full of constellations

how do you go from a savior to a stranger
with only a few words

deep in the depths of the sea
heavens above the horizon
there is a love that cannot compare to the one i feel for you

II.   lassitude

las·si·tude
/ˈlasəˌt(y)o͞od/
Noun

a state of physical or mental weariness; lack of energy.

i have become a specatator in my own life

we were on the same page
with different books in hand

do i want you
or the thought of you i created
as i layed awake staring at the ceiling
replaying those once vivid moments
over and over and over again
forgetting more of your flaws each time

if there was a rose for every thorn
i could handle the pain of being pricked each time i hold the flower

- *but the quantity of the roses could never amount to the quantity of the thorns*

is it not crazy
crazy that we live life as we would
and somebody steps into our lives
and it changes in an instant
we think about them when we work
when we eat
when we laugh
when we cry
we create movies in our minds of them while we sleep
we look at the stars wondering if they're look at the same
constellations
then just as quickly as they saved us
they tell us that they don't want you anymore
and our heaven turns to hell
the butterflies in our tummies fall dead and suddenly become a
million times heavier
our hearts drop to our ankles
our laughs turn to sobs
is it not crazy
that our lives can change
just because of a few words

the sun is beyond beautiful
but when you stare too long
your eyes begin to hurt
and the sun begins to blind you
so you look away
you try to appreciate another beautiful commodity
but still, all you see
is the sun
it will always take time
to be able to see the world as it is after you've looked at the sun too
long

- *beautiful things can still hurt*

she murdered the butterflies
just as quickly as she gifted them

did you bring light into my dim lit life
with the intention to walk away with more light than you came
with?

it is growing difficult to tell the difference between
freedom and loneliness

if they were worth waiting for
you wouldn't have to wait

- *reality check I*

so instead she satisfies herself with substance
the substance that wears off in a matter of hours
and leaves her stranded in reality
nothing is permanent

-    *reality check II*

friends don't let friends fall victim to themselves

-reality check III

i would rather feel the pain of losing you
than feel nothing at all

the comfortable feeling
of writing about the people that you love
knowing that they won't return anytime soon

a part of me wants to let you be so you wouldn't see what i've
become
but a part of me wants you to see how far i've come

you brought me to life only to kill me again

- *which hand held the medecine that would save me, and which hand held the medicine that would kill me?*

i drowned myself to save you
i resurfaced
only to see that it was you
holding my head under all along

24 hour chip
1 month chip
3 months chip
6 months chip
9 months chip

24 hour chip

-   *relapse*

the feeling of your touch is fading from my memory
i've forgotten what it feels like to breathe the same air as you

- *i'm not sure if i could recognize your laugh in a crowded room*

i am lost
i dont know where i am
i dont know who i am
don't try to look for me
do not send a search party
how can i be found
if i just keep running away

- *you could look all day and all night, but you can't save*
  somebody who isn't willing to save themself

the moment i heard those few words
the oceans of my infatuation ran dry

what about resistance
makes it so alluring

was it the alcohol
or the hands that grasp on to it as if it could grow legs and run
away
or was it the mouth that swallows it as if it was more necessary
than the air he breathes
could it be the mind that could only find salvation in the form of a
consumable liquid

- *which of these things took my father away from me first*

how do you expect me to go back to being your friend
how can you ask me to be your friend
after you've seen me in the ways you have
and after i've seen you in the ways i have

how can you replace the rain in my life with sunshine
only to replace it with a thunderstorm a few months later

how does he love *something* more than his own children
how does she love *someone* more than her own children

-   *your suicidal daughter*

where is the middle ground
when you want nothing at all
and i want everything and more

she dreams you meet again
on her next walk of life
one where your chapter never ends
the fantasy she was denied
you smiled sparks flew
you laughed her love grew
you spoke and she knew
that her love for you was true
she couldn't identify if she was in love with you
or the idea of you
she made up her mind
that you were one of a kind

so she made it clear
and you disappeared
she showed you what you meant to her
so unbothered as she hopes you treat the new one better

why do you need to be told that you're prettier than her
can't i tell you that you're pretty and let that be enough?

she made my wings
but i put them on
and learned how to fly

when you are telling her that you love her
you are teaching her
that love is violent
love is conditional
love is paralyzing
and as her father you should be teaching her
that love is beautiful
love is unconditional
love is kind
she will continue to grow with a negative understanding of what
those words mean
she has been taught to confuse rage with kindness

she now has to learn
to untangle the threads of deception
and understand how to recognize manipulation from healthy
affection

i find myself questioning why i can't see the world in black and white more times than i can count. i tell myself that things would be so much easier to understand. clearer. less difficult to interpret. then i open my eyes, i see that an achromatic world is not my reality. and i see the world around me. full of color, full of liveliness. i find quaint beauty in everything i come across. on occasion, i observe that beneath the surface level beauty, that is only available to the eye, i see the unattractive aspects of our actuality. i recall that if i only saw infinite shades of gray, that i wouldn't be able to appreciate the world for all that it is. contradicting, if i lived in a colorless world i would become blind to the unpleasant aspects of reality.

what do you mean when you say that i'm not acting like myself?

i am a flower
i have no control over my life
i depend on everybody else to take care of me
i can't move forward
i'm stuck in place
i can only move if somebody pushes me
people are okay with taking my life away from me
if it means they get to experience something beautiful for a short
moment

how old was she?

- *12-13*

how did she leave you
if she was never yours to begin with

how can you rip my heart out
and expect it to beat for you

they notice you when you are silently suffering
but they grow deaf when you scream for help

the first man to tell you he loved you
was the first man to tell you that you are less than
the first man to tell you that you will never amount to anything
above satisfactory

what do i have to do to reclaim my childhood as my own

who will i be after all my demons have been slayed

- *how do you even slay your demons*

my sisters perspective;

a daughter
is not supposed to die
before her mother

i was not meant
to be an only child

your name was not meant
to be a trigger

your face was not supposed
to be a sad sight

-   *if things were different*

you want to help and make a change
until you have to get off your ass and do something yourself

i can't tell if im trying to convince myself i don't love you
or if i'm trying to convince myself that i do

"i love you"
love is not abuse
"i love you"
love is not secrets, lies, and manipulation
"i love you"
love is not changing every detail about a person so they fit your standard of beauty

but what do *i* know about *love?*

how can i be my greatest enemy
but also be on the same team

   -   *self sabatoge*

i would swim the greatest oceans and climb the greatest mountains
to know that i was the reason you were smiling
one last time

i am not scared of the monsters hiding underneath my bed
rather
i am scared of the monsters hiding in the deepest corners of my
mind

it was on this day, in this moment that she realized
she was the villain in her own story

who the hell *would* i have been without you
who the hell *could* i have been without you

my body remembers what my mind forgets

ive died in a million different ways
but im still here breathing

- *that says something, doesnt it?*

"what doesn't kill you makes you stronger"

- *but a girl can only hurt so much until she meets her demise*

nobody likes depression
but i greet depression with a smile on my face
as i reach out to shake his hand

- *what about depression makes me feel so comfortable?*

every dream is a dream
until you wake up to find out it wasn't real
and i dissolves into a nightmare

III.   amour propre

   a·mour pro·pre
/ˌämoor ˈprôpr(ə)/
noun

   a sense of one's own worth; self-respect.

it does not make you a narcissist to love yourself

he tore the jewells from her crown
and shattered her gold to a million pieces
it was only as she chased the remnants trying to put them back
together
that she realized
her crown is not what made her a queen

she knows her worth
she is an imperfect, perfect creation

my body is not only the home of countless miracles. but she is a miracle within herself.

if
my
body
is
the
canvas
then
my
scars
are
art

i am learning to survive the storms of the world
but first i need to learn to survive the storms of myself

why would you want to be sunkissed
when you can *be* the sun?

be the force of nature
that intimidates the largest oceans and the brightest suns

- *they tremble at the sight of **you***

if i had nevery fallen to pieces
there would've been no cracks to fill with gold

why should a piece of glass determine how you feel about yourself?

what makes a mirrors opinion, more important than your own?

flowers grow from the marks on your body you call imperfections

every curve
every freckle
every beauty mark
every stretch mark
every bump
every edge
has been carefully hand shaped
into the perfect form it is today

and just as the caterpillar thought her life was coming to an end
she became a butterfly

while you are waiting for a knight in shining armour to come save you
he is busy saving himself
wishing you could do the same

there will always be something she has that you don't
and there will always be something that you have that she doesn't

- *you can't compare a fish who was destined to swim, to a bird who was destined to fly*

rather than being a liquid that takes the shape of any container it
finds itself in
be the air that roams freely and depends on nothing

no man
no woman
no person
is worth losing sight of who you are

learn the difference between want and need
and you will see the world in color

it took lifetimes
but now that my vision is clear
i can see that i deserved more

i raise mountains with my fingertips
and i create oceans at the sound of my song
my fuel is the love i feed to myself

i commit to myself

nothing can matter to you
until you matter to you

knowing your importance
and learning to love yourself
doesn't mean you can't have feelings for somebody
it doesn't mean that you have to do everything on your own
it just means that you have to have the will to walk away when you
need to
and the strength to ask for help

my hand is the only hand
that hovers above the light switch that controls the level of my
light

the satisfaction of saying "i love you" to the mirror
is unlike any other

i only learned to love myself
once i studied and accepted each of my flaws

power is the ability to fight
strength is knowing when to fight and when to watch

know who deserves your kindness based on who they are and what they do
nobody can convince you that they deserve you only through words

they told her she could not handle the fire
and she calmly replied to them
"i *am* the fire"

gift yourself the love that you've been searching for in others

stop saying sorry
for the scars on your body
you don't need to apologize
for not wanting to be alive
prove only to yourself
not anyone else
that you are worth the fight

for you are not your worst night

nobody deserves my breath
my heart
my time
or my love
more than i do

the growing pains that come with of leveling up

IV.   felicity

fe·lic·i·ty
/fəˈlisədē/
noun

intense happiness.

there will come a moment when you will turn and expect to feel
her gentle presence
and that will be when you see that she is gone for good

you are not your trauma
you are not lesser because of what people have done to you

knowing your worth is attractive

the person i used to be
is not a person i am proud of
but she is a person i had to be
in order for me become the person i am today

i have spent my entire life trying to find somebody to make me
whole
after meeting you
i now scc that i am a whole that perfectly compliments your whole

- *you should never need another person to make you feel all*
  that you are

~~im sorry that my love was too loud for somebody as small-minded as you~~

i am not apologetic for things i do not regret

healing isn't linear
healing isn't anything
healing is everything
there are no words to describe healing
healing moves every direction
up and down
left and right
back and forth
nobody knows what healing is because no person heals the same

it is not you coming up with the words
you are only the one putting them on paper
you are only the medium

my scars are ever lasting proof of my past
i am not proud
but i am not ashamed
i will embrace them
because they are now a part of me

you can miss the memories you made
without missing the person you made them with

i want to be the comfort you search for in times of despair
i want you to think of my touch when you need the extra support
i want to give you the feeling you give me
but as badly as i want this for myself
i will not love you until you can learn to love yourself
i want you to want me
but not until you've realized that you don't need me

i can install your training wheels
i can catch you when you fall
i can cheer you on
but at the end of the day
you are the only person who can learn to ride the bike

stay another day
with the hope that one day
things will be okay
what hurts today
hurts less than yesterday

you can't expect a table of one broken leg to hold a strong
foundation
you can't expect a support system of one healing woman to hold a
strong foundation

why do you care who i love
in what way does it effect your life

you can't look at them for who they *were* or who they *can be*
you have to look at them for who they *are*

does moldy fruit taste good, for the only reason that it was once
fresh?

there is strength found in the ability to identify what you need

how will you know if they are leaving you
or if they're walking at the same pace they always have been
and you're just standing in place

you can't put your life on pause for a person

holding on to the rope is okay
it means you're passionate enough to fight for your life
but when the rope begins to eat at the skin of your palms
the pain becomes unbearable
it is time to trust in the unknown
and to let go
because holding on when it hurts is not love

sometimes the tallest people fall
and the strongest people fold

a round of applause for the men and women
who survived and suffer in silence

you can't fix a broken society
you have to tear it all down
and rebuild it brick by brick

their disappearance was the worst thing that happened to you
but the best thing for you

part of me wishes things never changed

but *all* of me knows that i have to fully let go
to become who i need to be

i didn't have to learn how to escape my box
i only had to learn how to enter the world

the scars on your wrists and your thighs
the scars you cover with long sleeves and long pants
the horizontal ones the vertical ones
the deep ones the faded ones
the scars that you're embarassed of
those scars are only healing skin
those scars all have countless stories and feelings buried right
beneath the miscolored skin
so the next time you put makeup over them or wear long sleeves in
attempt to keep them a secret
Remember the stories and feelings behind them
and wear them with pride
because they will never define you
but they are a part of who you are

maybe the happy ending ive been waiting for was just me learning to move on

author's note

I wrote this book only to prove to myself that *it's okay to be afraid of the dark*, and as a means of expressing myself in a healthy way. I have published "*it's okay to be afraid of the dark*" with the intention of communicating to young women who have been, or are in my place, that they are not alone, and the intention of offering them a guide in their search self love. If you walk away with anything, I hope it is that you know, you are valuable. I hope you can walk away, understanding that you are more than your reflection could ever begin to describe to you. You are more than you think you are.

I have made remarkable progress, but I am not where I need to be. The way I was able to find my path, was through support, and hearing about the journey's my loved ones have travelled. So I am sharing my journey with you. *I am the reason* I have made so much progress, I am the one who got myself to where I am, but that was not without support. There are countless people in my life that have shown compassionate leadership, people that have taken my hand and allowed me to follow them along the path to healing. They did not save me. But they showed me the way, to save me, from me. Thank you to everybody who has had any sort of impact on who I am becoming. Thank you to Bryce Askew, Kaitlyn Finn, and Emily Johnsrud, for teaching me the distinction between kindness and compassion. For extending a guiding hand in my moments of vulnerability, and leading me along the path to finding myself, and for being the first people that have made me feel *seen*. Thank you to Meg Moss and Reed Hibbs, for showing me that there is goodness, for showing me that I am valuable, and for helping me understand that I am important and I am *loved*. Thank you to Rachael Cortner, Alicia Royer, Annie Royer, Alyssa Stokes, Dana Barqawi, Karen Naranjo, and everybody else that I have not mentioned, who has provided me with unconditional support. Today I am full of pride as I am able to say, that with help and with guidance, I am breathing, and that I am flourishing in a world that I once thought of as my enemy. *Life has become my reason, I have become my reason.*

it's okay to be afraid of the dark

charlotte guegan

CPSIA information can be obtained
at www.ICGtesting.com
Printed in the USA
BVHW070058291021
619737BV00001B/20